SCIENCE FICTION TO SCIENCE FACT

SOLAR SAILS

BY HOLLY DUHIG

Gareth Stevens
PUBLISHING

Please visit our website, **www.garethstevens.com.**
For a free color catalog of all our high-quality books,
call toll free 1-800-542-2595 or fax 1-877-542-2596.

Cataloging-in-Publication Data

Names: Duhig, Holly.
Title: Solar sails / Holly Duhig.
Description: New York : Gareth Stevens Publishing, 2018. | Series:
    Science fiction to science fact | Includes index.
Identifiers: ISBN 9781538214916 (pbk.) | ISBN 9781538213889
    (library bound) | ISBN 9781538214923 (6 pack)
Subjects: LCSH: Solar sails--Juvenile literature. | Space flight--
    Juvenile literature.
Classification: LCC TL783.9 D84 2018 | DDC 629.47'5--dc23

Published in 2018 by
Gareth Stevens Publishing
111 East 14th Street, Suite 349
New York, NY 10003

Written by: Holly Duhig
Edited by: John Wood
Designed by: Matt Rumbelow

Photo credits: Abbreviations: l-left, r-right, b-bottom, t-top, c-center,
m-middle. Images courtesy of Shutterstock.com. With thanks to Getty
Images, Thinkstock Photo and iStockphoto. Cover: bg – Raymond Cassel.
P4 – Andrey Armyagov. 5: t – Anelina; b – solarseven. 6: bg – solarseven;
bl – TTstudio. 7: tr – sdecoret; b – oneinchpunch; 8: bg – IM_photo; tr –
Kevin Gill/Flickr. 9: tr – NASA; bl – marmara4. 10: l – XYZ; r – Kirsanov
Valeriy Vladimirovich. 11: t – BrAt82. b – Alexyz3d. 12: t – Nicku; Tropical
studio. 13: t – Jen-nifer; b – NASA. 15: b – MarcelClemens; t – NASA.
16: tr – NASA. bl – Nostalgia for Infinity. 17: tr – Esteban De Armas; bl –
muratart. 18: bg – 3Dsculptor; tr – elenabsl. 19: tr – Andrey VP; bl – Paul
Fleet. 20: t – NASA; bl Alen Hunjet. 21 – solarseven. 22: Vadim Sadovski.
23: tr – NASA; Twin Design. 24: t – NASA; b – sdecoret. 25: bg – Stanislaw
Tokarski; br – adike. 26: tr – fluidworkshop bl – Lukiyanova Natalia
frenta. 27: lassedesignen. 28: tr – Vadim Sadovski. bl – Roman3dArt. 29:
tsuneomp. 30: 3000ad.

Printed in China

CPSIA compliance information: Batch CS18GS: For further information contact
Gareth Stevens, New York, New York at 1-800-542-2595.

SYSTEM
PROTECTION

LOGIN
PASSWORD

FIRST NAME
LAST NAME
HYSTORY: MISSING

DANGEROUS

3.52

1.41

CONTENTS

Words that appear like this can be found in the glossary on page 31.

SOLAR SAILS: THE FICTION

Imagine it's far in the future. You're excitedly sitting aboard some futuristic spaceship with your family. In a few hours, the spaceship will blast off and you will be on your way to explore strange, distant planets. You're going on a space vacation! As you look around, you can see all the normal parts of a spaceship. There's lots of complicated scientific equipment and even a special chair where the captain sits. But wait! Where are the huge, powerful rocket boosters that will carry you through space in a loud, fiery blaze?

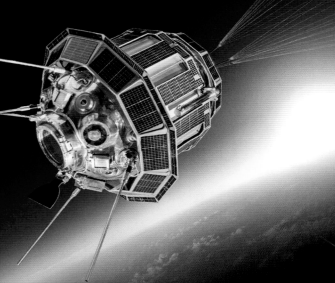

It turns out that making your way through the quiet, dark stretches of space might look very different in the future. Today's rocket **fuel** is very expensive and runs out quickly – just like the gas in a car. We need a different way to travel through the solar system. In the future, when you look out of your spaceship, you will finally see what is powering your ship. It is an enormous solar sail that will take you on your space vacation using the power of the Sun.

FROM VICTORIANS TO NOW

One of the first mentions of light-powered spacecraft came from Jules Verne's novel *From the Earth to the Moon*, way back in 1865! But although the idea has been around for a long time, you probably haven't seen many solar sails in science fiction. Usually everyone uses big rockets or futuristic warp drives. The humble solar sail doesn't get much attention at all. Still, they have shown up now and again in *Star Trek* and *Star Wars: Attack of the Clones*.

TIME TO SHINE

Well, it is time everybody knew about solar sails. Rocket ships are great, but these sails might be the future of space travel. Why, you ask? Well, rocket ships run on fuel and there are lots of problems with this. Let's take a look at a few of them…

SAILING AROUND THE SOLAR SYSTEM

Fuel is expensive. It takes an enormous amount of fuel to get one rocket out of the Earth's atmosphere. Traveling through the vacuum of space uses less fuel, but you will still have to take plenty with you so you don't run out. The more fuel you have, the heavier your spacecraft will be. The heavier your spacecraft is, the more fuel you'll need to fly it! This is getting complicated, isn't it? You can see why scientists are looking for another way.

Spacecraft fitted with solar sails are not able to get out of Earth's atmosphere on their own, so we will still need rockets to leave the planet. But rockets need fuel, and this becomes a problem in longer space missions.

ALTERNATIVES

So what else can we do? There are other options, such as using nuclear power. But, unlike solar sails, a lot of this technology is just not ready yet.

GRAVITY ASSISTS

Astronauts can save on fuel by using a **gravity** assist. Spaceships can fly near planets, moons, and stars and use their gravity to get a free speed boost.

As a planet like Jupiter **orbits** the Sun, it moves through space. If we can get a spacecraft close enough behind Jupiter as it speeds along, the spacecraft will be pulled along by the planet's gravity. This would be like if you were on roller skates being pulled by someone on a bike. You would be going a lot faster without having to do any work. As long as the spacecraft doesn't get too close, it will get a speed boost big enough to fly out into space.

When a spacecraft uses a planet's gravity to speed up, the planet will slow down a tiny, tiny bit. If enough spacecraft used a planet's gravity to travel, the planet could slow to a stop. If this were to happen, the whole planet would go flying into the Sun! But don't worry, it would take an enormous number of gravity assists before this happened.

SOLAR SAILS: THE REALITY

LIGHTSAIL

We don't have to imagine solar sails in the future – they already exist! One company has created a solar sail called LightSail. This solar sail wasn't carried far enough away to leave Earth's gravitational pull. However, it still worked well enough that they decided to make another, called LightSail 2.

Both sails were carried into space by a much bigger rocket using rocket fuel, but, after that, LightSail 2 should be able to travel on its own using the power of the Sun.

LIGHTSAIL 1 DID HAVE A FEW PROBLEMS WHEN IT LAUNCHED. THERE WAS A COMPUTER GLITCH THAT STOPPED IT WORKING. LUCKILY A COSMIC RAY FROM DEEP IN SPACE HIT LIGHTSAIL AND FIXED THE GLITCH.

THE EDGE OF THE EARTH'S ATMOSPHERE

SUNJAMMER AND NANOSAIL-D

America's space agency, NASA, wants to get involved with solar sails too. The first solar sail they sent into space was called the NanoSail-D. It orbited Earth for 240 days before coming back down and burning up in the atmosphere. NASA had plans for a second project called Sunjammer, which was going to be a much bigger sail. But this one never had a chance to sail the night sky, which is a shame because it had a much cooler name.

WHEN THE NANOSAIL-D WAS ORBITING EARTH, IT WOULD SOMETIMES REFLECT THE SUN'S LIGHT. IF YOU WERE LOOKING UP AT THE NIGHT SKY IN THE RIGHT PLACE AT THE RIGHT TIME, NANOSAIL-D WOULD HAVE LOOKED BRIGHTER THAN EVEN THE BRIGHTEST STARS IN THE NIGHT SKY.

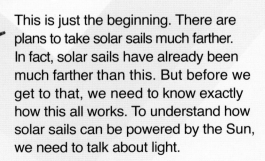

This is just the beginning. There are plans to take solar sails much farther. In fact, solar sails have already been much farther than this. But before we get to that, we need to know exactly how this all works. To understand how solar sails can be powered by the Sun, we need to talk about light.

PERHAPS SOLAR SAILS WILL BE ATTACHED TO BIGGER SPACECRAFT IN THE FUTURE, LIKE THIS.

WHAT IS LIGHT?

Light is a wave of energy. It is made up of a stream of particles called photons. These photons travel through the vacuum of space faster than anything else in the universe. Each ray of light has a wavelength. A wavelength is the distance between the same point on two waves, whether it be light waves, sound waves, or waves in the ocean. A short wavelength means the light wave has more energy. A wave of light with a long wavelength has less energy than a wave of light with a short wavelength.

SPECTRUM OF COLORS

The color of a ray of light depends on its wavelength. Red light has a longer wavelength, whereas blue light is shorter. If a ray of light has a wavelength longer than red, we can't see it any more. Long waves like these include infrared, radio waves, and microwaves, none of which we can see. On the other hand, if a ray of light has a wavelength shorter than violet, we also won't be able to see it. Ultraviolet light is a type of light beyond violet. Only some animals, such as bats, can see ultraviolet light.

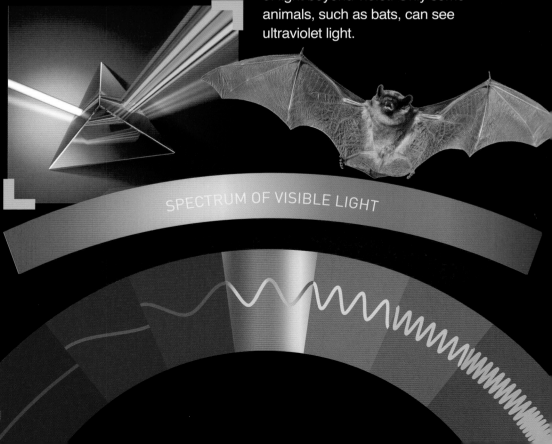

SPECTRUM OF VISIBLE LIGHT

BOUNCY PHOTONS

So now we know what light is, we can understand how solar sails work. The sails are like very big, thin mirrors that reflect light. When photons hit the sail, they are reflected and bounce back. As the photon bounces back, its energy gives the sail a small push. Of course, we wouldn't notice the effect of one photon, but the Sun constantly blasts out lots of them. The energy of all these photons together is what gives a solar sail speed.

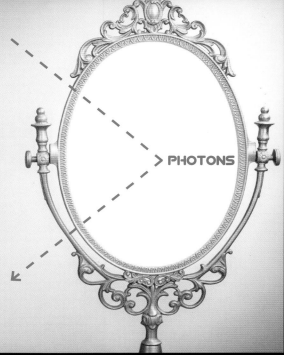

> PHOTONS

THE YARKOVSKY EFFECT

Stars radiate energy, which heats up any planets, moons, or asteroids that orbit them. Our Sun is a star, and we rely on its energy to keep us warm.

When a scientist named Ivan Yarkovsky studied asteroids, he found that a star's heat could affect an asteroid's path. Most asteroids rotate as they travel through space. If one side of an asteroid is warmed up by the Sun, soon that side will rotate and face away from the Sun. Now it is the asteroid's turn to radiate heat. The energy that radiates out into cold space pushes the asteroid in the opposite direction a tiny bit. But why did this radiation push the asteroid at all? To answer that question, we need to ask a man called Issac Newton.

THE SCIENCE OF SOLAR SAILS

ISAAC NEWTON

Many years ago, Newton came up with his three laws of motion. These are the basic rules that tell us how and why things move. For the most part, we still use them today. The only one we need to focus on right now is law number three. Could you remind us what that is, Newton?

FOR EVERY ACTION, THERE IS AN EQUAL AND OPPOSITE REACTION.

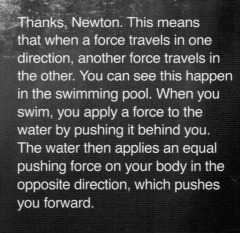

Thanks, Newton. This means that when a force travels in one direction, another force travels in the other. You can see this happen in the swimming pool. When you swim, you apply a force to the water by pushing it behind you. The water then applies an equal pushing force on your body in the opposite direction, which pushes you forward.

Do you see how important this is? This is why a rocket moves forwards when it applies a fiery force behind it. This is why an asteroid is slightly knocked off its path when it radiates heat. And this is why solar sails move forward when they reflect photons.

CHANGING DIRECTION

Gravity is an important part of how a solar sail changes direction. The planets orbit the Sun because of the Sun's gravity. Being in orbit is like being a ball attached to the pole in a game of tetherball. If our solar system was a gigantic game of tetherball, the Sun would be the pole, gravity would be the string, and planets would be the ball on the string. When planets orbit the Sun, they have enough speed to cancel out the pull of gravity. If they weren't moving so fast, they would fall into the Sun just like the ball would fall towards the pole in tetherball if you stopped hitting it. As long as nothing slows them down, planets will orbit the Sun forever.

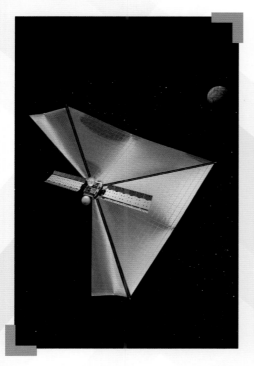

When a solar sail wants to travel round the solar system, it also orbits the Sun. But, depending on the angle of the sail, the spacecraft can move in different directions. In order to change their direction, solar sails turn off parts of their mirror sails so the photons are **absorbed** instead of reflected. By turning off the left side, for example, photons will only push on the right side. This causes the sail to rotate.

THE POWER OF THE SUN WILL BE GREATER THE CLOSER YOU ARE TO IT. THE FARTHER AWAY THE SAIL IS FROM A STAR, THE LESS PRESSURE FROM THE PHOTONS AND THE SLOWER THE SPEED.

ANGLES AND ORBITS

If a spacecraft tilts its sail so that it faces the Sun like in the first picture, the photons will push the spacecraft back. This way, a solar sail can move away from the Sun.

If a spacecraft wanted to move towards the Sun, it would angle its sail so that when the photons hit it, it would be pushed in the opposite direction to its orbit, like in the second picture.

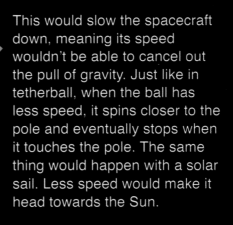

This would slow the spacecraft down, meaning its speed wouldn't be able to cancel out the pull of gravity. Just like in tetherball, when the ball has less speed, it spins closer to the pole and eventually stops when it touches the pole. The same thing would happen with a solar sail. Less speed would make it head towards the Sun.

PHOTONS

PUSH DIRECTION

ORBIT

OVERALL DIRECTION

IKAROS
FLYING TO VENUS

A solar sail called Ikaros detached itself from a rocket in space with a mission to fly to Venus all on its own. It was going to be the first spacecraft to travel around in space using only the power of the Sun.

Once it was in space, the next step for Ikaros was to spin around and unfurl its sail. About a month after launching, Ikaros detached little cameras to take a picture of itself and send it back to Earth. The picture showed that the sails had unfurled properly, meaning the spacecraft was ready for its journey. Later that year, Ikaros successfully flew past Venus. It is currently making its way back to us, but keeps slipping into hibernation mode due to lack of power. This is no time for sleep, Ikaros!

IKAROS, THE SLEEPY SOLAR SAIL, IS STILL OUT THERE SOMEWHERE.

IKAROS' SAILS ARE ONLY
0.0003 INCH THICK
(0.0075 MM), BUT ARE
46 FEET (14 M) WIDE.

NASA'S ASTEROID MISSION

We've already heard about NASA's Sunjammer and NanoSail-D, but it turns out that NASA isn't done with solar sails yet. NASA wants to find out about asteroids, so they are sending their Near-Earth Asteroid Scout (or NEA Scout for short) to investigate. Just like Ikaros, the NEA Scout will be folded up and attached to a bigger rocket. Once in space, it will detach and unfurl its sail, ready to travel to the asteroid.

The NEA Scout weighs around 31 pounds (14 kg) and the sail would be around 30 feet (9m) wide. The journey should take about two years, as long as nothing goes wrong. There is a robot attached to the sail about the size of a shoe box. It will be able to measure all sorts of things about the asteroid, such as how much it rotates and what it is made of.

THERE ARE MANY MYSTERIES ON THE SURFACE OF AN ASTEROID.

WHY DO WE NEED TO KNOW ABOUT ASTEROIDS?

There are lots of reasons to explore asteroids. One very good reason is that asteroids could be dangerous – especially the ones flying around near Earth. If an asteroid hit Earth, it could be pretty bad news for us, especially if the asteroid was big. In fact, it wouldn't be the first time a big asteroid collided with our planet: some scientists believe the last big one killed the dinosaurs. As you can imagine, scientists around the world are very eager to to stop something like that from happening again, so the more we know about asteroids, the better chance we have of stopping them.

THE DINOSAURS DIDN'T KNOW WHAT HIT THEM 65 MILLION YEARS AGO. WE WON'T MAKE THE SAME MISTAKE!

We don't exactly know where life came from and why. Some scientists think life may have formed around hot **vents** in the deepest depths of the ocean. Some think that life may have been helped by asteroids hitting the Earth. Maybe the only reason you are alive today and reading this book is because some asteroids carried the necessary material for life to begin and dumped it here on Earth. The only way to answer this mystery is to find out as much as we can about asteroids.

OTHER USES FOR SOLAR SA

AS SATELLITES

Let's say you want to send a satellite to orbit Earth. There are all sorts of reasons to do this. Satellites help us forecast the weather, communicate with phones, and use GPS to find our way around in cars. But here's the thing – Earth spins around as it travels through space, and a lot of these satellites that help us with phones and GPS need to orbit at the same speed as the Earth's spin. This is very difficult to do with normal satellites, so solar sails might just be our answer.

By attaching a solar sail to a satellite and tilting it to a certain angle, you could give it the powe needs to move at the same spee as the Earth's spin. This means we would have lots more useful satellites. GPS for everyone!

VACUUM CLEANER

There are over 19,000 pieces of debris orbiting somewhere around Earth that are bigger than 4 inches (10 cm) across. Some of this stuff is flying around Earth at up to 6 miles per second (10 km/s). This is pretty dangerous for satellites and astronauts. All this debris mostly comes from old rockets and satellites that have no way of getting back down. There are lots of broken satellites up there, and we are going to need a way of getting them down, or at least stopping them from breaking anything in the future.

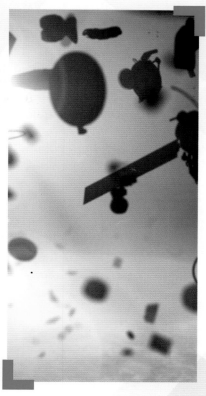

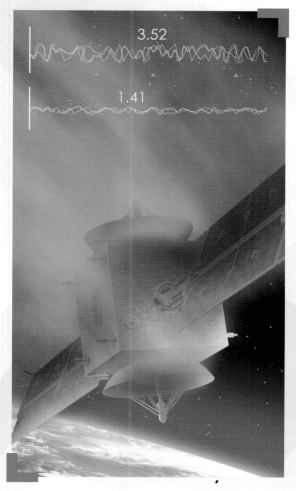

If a solar sail was attached to a satellite, it would act as a brake and slow the satellite down. Do you remember what happens when an object loses speed in an orbit? Gravity makes it fall towards the thing they are orbiting, which – in this case – is Earth. The sail and satellite would then burn up as they entered the atmosphere and wouldn't be clogging up space any more.

Maybe one day we will invent a satellite that collects space debris. Once it has collected all the debris, a solar sail could be used to drag it back to Earth, burning it all up safely.

BEYOND THE SOLAR SYSTEM

Clearly solar sails have plenty to do in the near future, whether that is orbiting Earth or traveling to different asteroids and planets in our solar system. But what will we do when we've explored everything nearby? One day we are going to want to go farther into space, to other stars and solar systems. But, compared to rockets, solar sails are slow, and they only get slower when they get farther away from a star. If we're going to explore planets orbiting another star, we better find a way to speed things up!

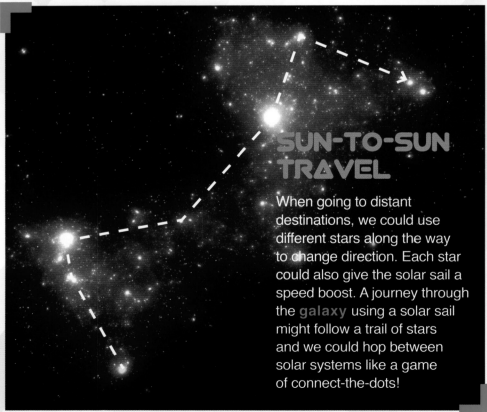

SUN-TO-SUN TRAVEL

When going to distant destinations, we could use different stars along the way to change direction. Each star could also give the solar sail a speed boost. A journey through the **galaxy** using a solar sail might follow a trail of stars and we could hop between solar systems like a game of connect-the-dots!

LASERS

But what do you do when your solar sail is far away in space and there are no nearby stars? Well, you could provide the energy yourself! Using a high-powered laser, you could shine a beam of photons right at the sail, propelling it forwards. Unlike the Sun, which emits photons in all directions, a laser puts all of its photons in one spot. And if that spot is a solar sail, you could keep a spacecraft going no matter how far away it gets.

THE PROBLEMS WITH LASERS

Unfortunately, it is not possible to power solar sails with lasers at the moment. The laser would need a lot of energy – some people think it would use as much energy as the whole world put together. Also, the farther away solar sails get, the harder it is to aim the laser beam at the sails. It is very easy to miss something that is millions of miles away. But although there are a lot of drawbacks to using lasers today, this idea might still be possible in the future.

E-SAILS

A NEW TYPE OF SAIL

Scientists are always working on something new. Scientists at NASA are already looking into a new type of solar sail called an electric sail, or e-sail. The electric sail also gets its power from the Sun, but it does so in a different way.

SOLAR WIND

The Sun doesn't just throw out energy in the form of light. It's got a few more tricks up its sleeve. The Sun is constantly chucking out a stream of charged particles that we call solar wind. These particles are either positive or negative. Particles with different charges move towards each other. Particles with the same charge bounce away from each other if they get too close.

THE CHARGED PARTICLES ARE THROWN FROM THE SUN AT VERY HIGH SPEEDS. THEY CAN BE AS FAST AS 435 MILES (700 KM) PER SECOND.

SO HOW DO ELECTRIC SAILS WORK?

Instead of having a giant mirror, electric sails would have a fan of thin wires around the spacecraft that form a circle. These wires would be kept positively charged. When the charged particles from the solar wind hit the e-sail, the positive particles would bounce off the positive wires. This would push the e-sail forwards. Both e-sails and solar sails get their fuel from the Sun, and both bounce particles off their sail in order to move. Hopefully NASA will get an e-sail working soon, because it would be a lot faster than a solar sail.

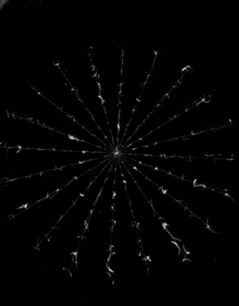

SOLAR FLARES

Sometimes energy can build up in the Sun and be released as a solar flare. A solar flare is a burst of photons and charged particles. These can be quite dangerous for nearby planets because solar flares can strip away their atmosphere. But for solar sails and e-sails, solar flares might be useful. All the extra photons and charged particles would give them a huge speed boost.

LUCKILY, EARTH ISN'T BADLY DAMAGED BY THESE SOLAR FLARES, BUT IT CAN AFFECT OUR SATELLITES.

MISSION: STARSHOT

Some scientists have already set their sights on the other stars. By using solar sails, the famous scientist Stephen Hawking and his team want to send tiny **probes** to the nearest solar system to ours, Alpha Centauri. This mission is called Starshot. Alpha Centauri is a collection of three stars, the smallest of which is called Proxima Centauri. Proxima Centauri is a red dwarf. Red dwarfs are much smaller, cooler stars than our Sun. However, the probes aren't interested in Proxima Centauri – they are interested in a planet that orbits it, called Proxima b.

PROXIMA B IS AROUND 4.2 LIGHT-YEARS AWAY. THE STARSHOT PROBES ARE MEANT TO GET THERE IN 20-30 EARTH YEARS.

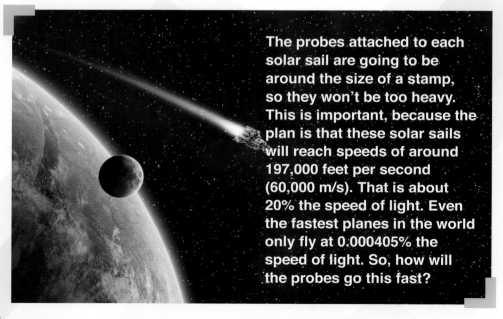

The probes attached to each solar sail are going to be around the size of a stamp, so they won't be too heavy. This is important, because the plan is that these solar sails will reach speeds of around 197,000 feet per second (60,000 m/s). That is about 20% the speed of light. Even the fastest planes in the world only fly at 0.000405% the speed of light. So, how will the probes go this fast?

BIGGER LASERS

Starshot's solar sails will be propelled through space by powerful lasers. Because the probes are so light, it would take a lot less energy to get them moving. That's the idea, anyway. When the probes get to Proxima b, they will use their tiny, lightweight equipment to take pictures of the planet and hopefully find out all sorts of things, such as what it is made from, exactly how big it is, and if it has been damaged by the red dwarf's solar wind.

This mission won't happen any time soon, though. Everything is still being studied to make sure it will actually work in real life. If everything goes to plan, we will receive pictures of Proxima b in the year 2060.

You might be wondering why we would go to so much effort to visit this far-off planet. Well, this planet is in what scientists call the habitable zone, which means it could possibly be home to alien life! You're excited now, aren't you?

PROBES ARE SENT OUT TO INVESTIGATE PLACES FAR AWAY. THE SOLAR SAIL PROBES GOING TO PROXIMA B WILL BE A LOT SMALLER THAN NORMAL PROBES.

HABITABLE PLANETS

HABITABLE ZONE

When we say habitable zone, we are talking about a planet being a certain distance away from its Sun so that water can form on its surface. If a planet is too close to its Sun, like Mercury is to our Sun, it is too hot for water to form. Too far away, like Neptune, and all the water would be frozen. Because it orbits a small red dwarf, Proxima b is a lot closer to its star than Earth is to our Sun.

BEING CLOSER MEANS IT TAKES LESS TIME FOR THIS PLANET TO ORBIT ITS STAR. A YEAR ON PROXIMA B IS ONLY 11 DAYS LONG.

WHAT DOES LIFE NEED TO SURVIVE?

The truth, is we don't know what life needs. There may be aliens out there that eat fire or don't need oxygen to breathe. But we do know that life on Earth needs things like water and air. As far as we know, all life will need these things, so we need to look for Earth-like planets. Even though Proxima b might be Earth-like in some ways, there are all sorts of problems it could have. That's why we need to get a closer look.

Still, even if we get to Proxima b and only find a bunch of fiery, lifeless rocks, that doesn't mean we have to give up hope. Scientists think there are at least a billion Earth-like planets in our galaxy that may be able to support life. With all those planets, there must be life somewhere. So why is it so quiet out there in the universe?

Lots of people have tried to come up with an answer for why we haven't already seen aliens if there are so many other planets. Here's a few ideas:

- LIFE IS VERY RARE, SO THERE AREN'T MANY ALIENS OUT THERE TO TALK TO OR VISIT.

- INTELLIGENT ALIENS INVENT COOL STUFF AND HAVE SUCH NICE LIVES THEY DON'T WANT TO LEAVE THEIR PLANET.

- COMPARED TO THE WHOLE UNIVERSE, HUMANS HAVEN'T BEEN AROUND FOR VERY LONG, SO WE JUST NEED TO WAIT A LITTLE LONGER.

- ALIENS ARE TOO SCARED TO TALK IN CASE THERE ARE OTHER, NASTY ALIENS OUT THERE WHO WILL DESTROY THEM.

Why do you think we haven't heard from aliens yet?

INTERSTELLAR SAILING TRIPS

A JOURNEY FOR HUMANS

We've looked at probes and robot spacecrafts using solar sails, but what about people? The kind of spacecraft that could carry people would be heavy and slow because people need a lot of stuff to stay alive and comfortable. This doesn't mean it won't happen in the future, but it does mean that solar sail journeys would be very long indeed for humans.

SUSPENDED ANIMATION

Future space journeys across the galaxy could take hundreds of years. This is a problem. Your pilot won't be very good at steering the spacecraft when they've died of old age. In science fiction, people solve this problem using something called suspended animation. This is where a person is frozen in a special chamber and doesn't age until years later when they are woken up and thawed out. So after you hop onboard your spaceship, you would climb inside your chamber and set your alarm to wake you up in a hundred years. Unfortunately, in real life we have no way of waking a frozen person up... yet.

HUMAN COLONY

A much more practical solution to the problem of long-distance space travel is to set up a floating human **colony**. This is a spaceship carrying hundreds or thousands of people. None of these people will actually see the stars and planets they are traveling to, but their great-great-great grandchildren will. A human colony is like a big town slowly journeying through space. It would have all the things that we would need to survive, like farms, houses, and lots of solar panels to provide electricity. It might also be powered by an enormous solar sail.

A spaceship like this would have to create its own gravity and daylight. Everything would be recycled, even air and water. People would still have families and children would still go to school. There would be normal things like stores and parks. Eventually the colony would be full of people that weren't even born when the journey started. Then one day, the spaceship would finally reach its destination and the colony would begin to build towns and cities on their new planet.

SOLAR SAILS: THE FUTURE

So in the future, when you are waiting for your space vacation to begin, you'll know all about the massive solar sail fixed to the spacecraft. You can impress your family with your newfound knowledge.

But you haven't told us where you're going. Are you off to Mars? You could visit Olympus Mons, the tallest volcano in the solar system, which is twice as big as Mount Everest. Maybe you are going to Titan, one of Saturn's moons? Titan has huge lakes of liquid methane and a great view of the rings of Saturn. Is it Neptune, the farthest planet from our Sun? Scientists think that it rains diamonds there. Or maybe you are just going for a sail around the solar system. Who can blame you? It sounds like a nice way to travel, don't you think?

GLOSSARY

absorbed	taken in or soaked up
asteroids	rocky and irregularly shaped objects that orbit around the Sun
atmosphere	the mixture of gases that make up the air and surround the Earth
colony	a group of people living in a foreign or distant place
communicate	to pass on information
cosmic ray	energetic particles traveling through space near to the speed of light
debris	scattered pieces of rubbish
fuel	something that can be used to produce energy or power
galaxy	many solar systems, stars, and planets that all orbit around a central point, usually a black hole
gravity	the force that pulls everything downwards towards the center of the Earth
habitable	capable of being lived in
hibernation	in a dormant state
light-years	a measurement based on how far light travels in a year; one light-year is 5.8 trillion miles (9.5 trillion km)
nuclear power	energy created by splitting atoms apart
orbits	an object following a path around a larger object in space
particles	extremely small pieces of a substance
probes	types of spacecraft designed to explore other planets and send back information
satellite	a machine in space that travels around planets, taking photographs and collecting and transmitting information
thawed	unfrozen and warmed up
vacuum	a space devoid of matter
vents	an opening that allows air, gas, or liquid in or out

INDEX